BEHIN... E
I HAVE THE FACE OF SKELETOR

Petrol Honey

Rob Auton
Illustrated by the Author

Burning Eye

Also available by Rob Auton:

Try your best, but don't take yourself too seriously.

Cricket commentator

Dear Reader,

Just a quick note about the writing that appears in this book. The writing that appears in this book was written to be read out loud to strangers. Some of the writing in this book, such as this, has never been read out loud to strangers. It is by no means crucial to read the writing in this book out loud to strangers but if you do get the opportunity to read the writing in this book out loud to strangers please grab the opportunity with the hand that isn't holding this book.

Ideal environments to read the writing in this book at the top of your voice include:

1. On a really busy but quiet in volume tube train when your mouth is really near someone's face.

2. In an interview situation when the interviewer asks you what you know about the company.

3. At a wedding directly after somebody has repeatedly struck a glass with a knife.

There are, of course, lots of other opportunities that may arise when you think the time is right to read the writing in this book out loud but please keep the above suggestions in mind as a starting point.

This book can also be read without reading the writing out loud as you are probably doing now.

Thanks for reading this writing.

All the best,

Rob

Remember

Remember could have been a good name for a month
The month of Remember
A month that comes after December but before January
When people are given a month off work to sit down and
remember
To remember what they have done and haven't done
over the course of the year
But how would people remember that there is a new month?
Possibly with the rhyme
Remember, remember the month of Remember
A four week period for people to breathe
To look
To stop
To remember
To remember that we are alive
To remember that we were dead before we were born and that
is what death might feel like
The month of Remember could never be
It would take too much organising
Maybe the word of remember is enough
Enough for us to remember

Thumbs

My thumbs are wet and it's not working.

Well what are you trying to work?

I don't know, just life I guess.

Well why don't you dry your thumbs and see if your life gets any better?

I can't find anything to dry them on.

Here look you can use my T-shirt if you like?

Are you sure?

Yes.

You won't mind having a little bit of wet on your T-shirt?

Not if it makes your life better.

Why are you so nice to me?

I want you to have dry thumbs and to be there when they get wet and nothing works.

Growing Silence

It is March outside
It is March inside as well
That is how months work
They get into everything
Even down the smallest hole it is March
Time fits perfectly into the corners
Fills the gaps between the hairs on my arms
Leaves on trees are only just making it possible for people to say

There are leaves on the trees

Leaves are so silent when they are new and small
Like human babies in the womb
But they are on branches
As the year goes on they grow larger and louder
If the wind is playing them right
You can hear them in the trees
Just being leaves
When a leaf drops to the pavement
It might make a tiny impact sound
Later maybe a gentle scraping as the wind blows it slightly along
It will be a leaf for a bit longer
Making fewer and fewer sounds
Eventually falling into silence forever

One Creature Zoo

Looking down from my bedroom window
I saw it moving in my next door neighbour's garden
The tortoise that slowed down my heart
I stood, excited and relaxed all at once
A visual brain massage with a shell
How long had it been breathing for?
Had it seen the Second World War?
Walking the grass of the London lawn
Protected by its permanent strapless army hat
When the air raid sirens came, was the tortoise carried to safety?

Two winters ago I saw the elderly couple pick the slow motion
one up, put it in a cardboard box full of straw and set the garden
shed dial to hibernate
It looked like a one man job but they both had roles
One holding the door as the other carefully carried the tortoise
into the wooden dark
I would look at the closed shed and think about the slow sleeper
Head in its shell
Head in its shelter
Wondering if it had its eyes shut
What do tortoises dream about?
I hope they don't have nightmares
I think humans deserve the terror sometimes
A tortoise, however, should be able to rest in a winter world
of fresh, clean, sure of shape leaves
Iceberg sky with rocket clouds

Just as those almost-same-as-head feet had stepped out of the
back of my mind
The bike of spring arrived with the being in its basket
I pointed down at it and felt like I should ring somebody
But the wonder wouldn't have got through

I saw the tortoise on just one other occasion that year
In the middle of the small square lawn
The elderly man standing over it with a smile
I remember seeing them in the sunshine
A man at one with his pet
A perfectly silent relationship
Autumn came and the lights got nighter
I must have missed the hibernation ceremony
On Christmas Day I knew where the tortoise would be

Spring grew into view once more
As the nights got lighter
I looked out for the tortoise
But it didn't appear
One Saturday morning I looked down onto the garden
Amongst three garden gnomes sat a stone statue of a tortoise
A rectangular metal plaque on the side of its shell
Too far away to read but not to understand
It sits there as still as the tortoise used to
Hibernating forever in the sometimes warm stone of time

FORT FOR THE DAY

THE ELEPHANT CAN'T MOVE BECAUSE HIS LEGS ARE THE GAPS

Smoke

Sitting at the top of a tall tree in America somewhere
There is snow on the ground below that nobody has stepped in
I guess I have been up here for quite a long time
I don't feel tired
I must have been asleep
Quite an achievement to have fallen asleep in a tree
And not fallen out
A canary just landed on my shoulder
Its feet are surprisingly cold
I didn't think they were big enough to get cold feet
Am I happier up here in this make-believe tree
Than I am in reality?
I have to imagine the snow covered branches here
If I want to smell something I have to make it up
Smoke
I just looked up from my desk and out of the window
I saw a woman dressed in a red coat eating an apple
I didn't have to imagine it
She did all the hard work for me

Heaven Food

What's the food like in Heaven?
If all well-behaved living things that die go to Heaven
Can there be meat up there?
Do people imagine eating nice bits of meat in Heaven?
You know, the bits with a tiny bit of burnt on the cliff face of fat
Sitting at a solid square legged without wobble table
Eating a steak with a smooth heavy shining fork
and a deep dark brown wooden handled steak knife
Has the cow that the steak came from died and gone to Heaven
only to be killed again?
Do they kill dead cows up there so we can eat meat and really
be in total Heaven?
What about the sandwiches? Are there crumbs in Heaven?
Can you get Lurpak? Is it complimentary?
Do you still have to peel oranges?
Do apples have cores or are they all apple? Can you eat right
through an apple from one side to the other? Can you eat an
apple until it is gone? Where do apples go when they die?
Do baked beans come in tins or do they float into your open
mouth in a kind of horizontal unfastened necklace line of
warm non drip perfectly cooked baked beans?
Where do I go to get my food when I arrive?
I will probably need to do a big shop
Or will all my cupboards be full?
Will I have cupboards? Who will have put them up?
Does God put the cupboards up in Heaven?
All the chickens will be running around laughing and kissing
instead of lying dead and refrigerated in the supermarket
Do people kill chickens in Heaven?
Maybe the chickens kill themselves and roll around in
breadcrumbs for us?
Maybe the chickens get to go up to the next level of Heaven
The Heaven of Heaven
The penthouse suite of Heaven
If you have a fly in your kitchen in Heaven and you want to
get rid of it, what do you do?
You have both been accepted into Heaven

Roundabout

Walking up the road
For some reason I looked up
A crow flew directly above me
Black as a crow
Shadow strapped to its underside
Neck and neck
One neck blessed with feathers
One neck blessed with neck
When we reached the roundabout the crow stopped
Did its best impression of a funeral bound hummingbird
Gave way to a starling from the right
There were dozens of birds making traffic of themselves
A raised roundabout laid from flight
When it was clear the crow flew round the roundabout
Took the third exit and continued on its journey
As the crow doesn't fly

Roses And Cream

A dozen red roses tied to a Margate seafront
Someone's in love with the water
Or are they flowers of thanks?
Roses of remembrance perhaps?
Looking at them I remember that roses don't grow in the sea
Neither do strawberries
I would like to go strawberry picking in the sea
Exercise my way out to sweet wet wonder
In a wooden rowboat
Salt water wouldn't work
Give me a double cream sea
Oar ends dripping with slow white
One of the world's worst whisks
Leaning over the side to pick from the what would be
waveless surface
Where shall we go for pudding?
The sea

Human Wolves

That fear sits in me like a settee I am scared of
In my chest at the front
Stagnant danger
Brown and hairy
I can't make out their faces
Only the blurs of their shapes
Dark soft outlines against the white through the wardrobe
Narnia inspired nightmares
In the childhood of Yorkshire daytime
An ability to haunt before death
The directed wolves that taught me how to be frightened
To be frightened of something that isn't real

Skeleton Under My Skin

The following piece came about as I was asked to write a ghoulish
porn story to accompany an exhibition of ghoulish porn art. This is
not based on a true story or any experiences I have had in my life. If
you are under the age of eighteen it might be an idea to ask an adult
to read it first to see if this story is suitable for you to read.

I sit in the back room of an almost empty candlelit Soho
restaurant. An elderly Italian man plays the piano as I sit at a
table for two with the skeleton of a mermaid. She is wearing a
blonde wig that gives her the look of a dead for years Pamela
Anderson. On her face is the same expression that all skulls
possess: surprised to be dead. Her lower half lies under the
square table, a fish stripped of its scales and meat. Her tail has
a stereotypical fish skeleton, apart from the fact that she has
covered it with PVA glue and sprinkled it with silver and gold
glitter. Twinkling in the dull light of the tablecloth canopy, it
is a sky under there and tonight we eat from the floor of the
universe.

I watch mesmerised as the Rioja falls down her once throat, the
trickle lightly splattering her ribs reminding them of blood. The
ruby ribbon of liquid briefly disappears behind her loose fitting
emerald corset until it puddles on the cushion of her seat.

She lifts two full golf ball sized tomatoes from her salad to her
eye sockets and screws them into position. Bursting as she does
so, red plasma coated seed tears slide slowly down the white of
what used to be her cheeks. Green star vine connectors sit in
place of pupils, I am aroused by this and that was her aim.

A skeletal tail plays footsie with me under the censorship of the
table. Moving up my leg it scrapes at my shins with my shoelaces
caught in its racer-spoke like points. I feel the blood begin to
soak into my jeans and take a deep breath. I do not recoil. This
is why we are in a relationship. Nobody else has this.

Taking a lipstick from her handbag she removes the gold cap with difficulty, struggling to grip the metal with the tips of her bone. Eventually taking it to her ancient browning teeth she bites at it. The clink of her sound gives me goose bumps and makes me realise how quiet flesh covered humans are compared to skeletons. When a living person picks up a glass it is almost silent. When a skeleton does it, there is a substantial amount of sound. She twists slowly and paints the white around her mouth red. No lips to stick.

I still don't know her name. It has never come up in conversation. A question that will be neither asked nor answered. She takes the lipstick lid and drops it on the floor on purpose. It hits the carpet like a slow motion bullet shell in a big budget action movie. A single skeletal finger rises to her hollow mouth. Whoops, she whispers in an accent that you develop when you go to Heaven.

Bending down to the floor to retrieve the lid, she disappears under the table.

The sound of the ocean fills my ears as she undoes my fly. There is no tongue, only teeth. No moisture, only dust. I focus on the flame of the candle on top of the piano and try not to look at the couple on the table to our right. They have been discussing the rise in tube fares for the past half hour. I listen to their concerns as the teeth of the skeleton of the mermaid bring me to climax. With my hands gripped onto the corners of the table I thrust and shoot my life into her death. Her tomato eyes drop from their sockets into my groin, punctured and used.

ARE YOU THE ORANGUTAN WHO SAYS "YES" ALL THE TIME?

NO.

Tourist

Sometimes when I'm walking on my own in London
I like to wear my rucksack on my front
It transforms me into a tourist
A tourist in the city I have lived in for nine years
Not only does it transform me into a tourist
But a tourist who is ON HIS OWN
People look at me as I walk solo along the Southbank
They must think I am very brave to come to London
unaccompanied
I see parents pointing me out to their children
Look Billy, he must be an explorer
I pretend to see things for the first time
But act the same way I always do
St Paul's
Just look up

The Bus Office

This is my office! This is my office! said the man on the bus excitedly.
Look! This is one of my office windows! he said, stroking the bus window.
He was touching the wet, the liquid from the lives of London.
The person sitting next to him had her headphones on.
He began to press the red stop button as if it were an emergency.
Ooh I think I've got a new answerphone message!
Yes thought so, did you hear the beep?
The bus stopped at the next stop.
I told you I had a message, look at it out there.
The man pointed to the queue of people getting onto the bus.
My new message will be here soon and I will be able to hear
my new message. Look at my new message coming into my office.

A lady behind him leaned forward and said,
We are people, not your answerphone messages.

What was that? Have you got a message for me?

I haven't got a message for you, said the lady.

Is that your message? That I haven't got a message?
I have no new messages? Look at all these messages.
I think you will find I've got loads of messages.
I'm a busy man.

Bubble Wrap Warp

I found a large roll of big bubble bubble wrap under my bed. I couldn't remember buying it and had never seen it before. It was heavier and more colourful than the bubble wrap I was used to. On closer inspection I realised that contained in each bubble was a day of my life. A back catalogue bubble calendar of my time spent on Earth. I carefully carried the roll through into my living room and unrolled it on the floor. Starting at the top left hand corner of the metre high rolled out roll, I took a magnifying glass and peered into the first bubble to see the scene of my birth. Putting my ear to it I could just about hear my own primal scream. Following the days along the rows, cine film memories of homemade paddling pools, I saw my Mum and Dad at the age I am now. Gravity forced my jaw to drop as I watched myself take my first steps. I gently stroked this bubble of development with the tip of my index finger, never had I wanted to pop anything less. The half spheres of my life went on, some bubbles simply a colour, overcast grey dots or bright yellow holiday bubbles. Candles of birthday cakes just far enough away from the dome roofs to stop them from smouldering. I saw my years line up and began to seek out particular events. The first time my Dad took me fishing, seeing a float go under, him instructing me to strike triggered thoughts of ten pin bowling with my friends from school. A bird's eye view of my driving test from start to finish. A bubble full of northbound train next to a darkly clothed funeral bubble. The tip of the Eiffel Tower almost piercing my Parisian memory. Full stop sized flashing lights shone from miniature festival stages. The cellophane vibrated against my fingerprints as I tried to figure out which gig was which.

Some bubbles hot with food, others cold with frost. The bubbles allowed me to see my life as some sort of poster. I wondered if I should have filled the bubbles with a different life? Should the piece be more exciting? Particular bubbles look so packed it's as if they were twice as full as others. Hangover bubbles. Break up bubbles.

I watched my life develop in these free of snow snow globe scenes until I reached the last full bubble that showed me typing this. The bubbles after it are empty. They sit waiting for me to climb into tomorrow's plastic. To fill tomorrow with my life. It is up to me to prevent it from being a wet beige overcast blocked sink of a day. To fill it with something I can look back on. I began to think about other people's bubble wrap strips. How everyone on Earth has their own individual piece. Bubbles filled with dancing and murder. Cooking and building. Sleeping and jumping. Roast beef. Marbles. Duvets. Blue television screens through windows. A hollow can tumbleweeding down the floor of a nearly at its destination night bus. Brand new clean gravel fish tanks. Washing and zipping. Living and dying. We walk coated in the bubble wrap sheets of our past, protecting us as we travel into the future.

Jumpers

Lying face down on my single bed
Wearing my brand new white woolly jumper
It had the words I AM ON MY OWN!
Knitted in large black block capital letters on the front
There was a knock at my bedroom door
DO NOT COME IN HERE, I shouted
I quickly took off my new jumper and put on my old red cardigan
The white text on the red read, I AM NOT ALONE!
I answered the door
My friend came in wearing a plain black sweatshirt
She was a mystery to me

Sound Age

A fire engine siren started up
NEEEEEEEEE
I expected the NOR
But the NEEEEEEEE just kept coming
NEEEEEEEEEEEEEEEEEEEEEEEEEEEEEEEEEEEEEEEEEEEEE
Where was the NOR?
Where had the NOR gone?
We need the NOR
We need the NOR
What do we need?
The NOR
We need the NEE too, but you can't just have half a siren
Half a siren is no good to anybody
What is the NEE without the NOR?
NEEEEEEEEEEEEEEEEEEEEEEEEEEEEEEEEEEEEEEEEEEEEEE
Louder and higher and sharper went the NEE
NEEEEEEEEEEEEEEEEEEEEEEEEEEEEEEEEEEEEEEEEEEEEE
EEEEEEEEEEEEEEEEEEEEEEEEEEEEEEEEEEEEEEEEEEEEEE
EEEEEEEEEEEEEEEEEEEEEEEEEEEEEEEEEEEEEEEEEEEEEE
EEEEEEEEEEEEEEEEEEEEEEEEEEEEEEEEEEEEEEEEEEEEEE
EEEEEEEEEEEEEEEEEEEEEEEEEEEEEEEEEEEEEEEEEEEEEE
EEEEEEEEEEEEEEEEEEEEEEEEEEEEEEEEEEEEEEEEEEEEEE
EEEEEEEEEEEEEEEEEEEEEEEEEEEEEEEEEEEEEEEEEEEEEE
EEEEEEEEEEEEEEEEEEEEEEEEEEEEEEEEEEEEEEEEEEEEEE
EEEEEEEEEEEEEEEEEEEEEEEEEEEEEEEEEEEEEEEEEEEEEE
EEEEEEEEEEEEEEEEEEEEEEEEEEEEEEEEEEEEEEEEEEEEEE
EEEEEEEEEEEEEEEEEEEEEEEEEEEEEEEEEEEEEEEEEEEEEE
EEEEEEEEEEEEEEEEEEEEEEEEEEEEEEEEEEEEEEEEEEEEEE
There was nooo NOOOOOOR to be heard
Windows of nearby buildings committed suicide by jumping
from their frames
People on the pavements rocked in the foetal position
Hands blindfolded ears
Hours passed, then days, then months, then years
Sound then did to life on Earth
What ice had done many years before

Dog

When I was little I didn't know what a dog was
It didn't stop me from liking them
I feel the same way now
What is a dog?
I could draw you an outline on a piece of paper
Or point one out to you in the street
That doesn't mean I know what a dog is
I could look it up and read what people have written
That doesn't mean they know what a dog is
What is a dog?
A dog has hair
I have hair
Am I a dog?
No
Why not?
I got lucky
Did I?
In some ways
Which ways?
I'm not sure

IF
LOVE
HAD
LEAVES
AT LEAST WE WOULD
KNOW WHEN
IT WAS DYING

Dolphin

Inflatable, plastic, pound shop dolphin
Floating on your four cornered chlorine sea
If you were flesh and bone
Would you be smiling as much as you are now?
Would you feel as inflated?
Would your eyes be as wide with the bulge of optimism?
You have been surprised ever since I filled you with the
contents of my lungs
My breath, your invisible warm dolphin blood
I tell myself an inflatable plastic pound shop dolphin
Is still a dolphin
Look at you, walking on water in your own discounted way
My some sort of blown up magic Jesus fish
Do you like swimming with humans?
I saw the dolphin list of the top 100 things to do before you
die recently
Swim with humans wasn't on it
Maybe you don't enjoy our company as much as we think
you do?
I don't know what will happen to you if I stop going
swimming
You don't see many inflatables in second-hand shops

The Cartoon Of Reality

Existence is a cartoon train ride I am desperately holding on to the front of the train frantically laying track I speed into what seems like inevitable disaster grabbing bits of wood and metal that seem to come from nowhere trying to give myself some sort of future to travel on I travel into the unknown desert of time I haven't watched slip by yet not knowing where the next bit of track is going to come from never mind thinking about which direction I am going in blindly attempting to...

I'm sitting comfortably in a food filled tapas bar
Those small green peppers
With the nice salt on
That I can't remember the name of
Red wine in bricky small handleless mug cups
Blood of a beautiful moment
Lamb chops from the best cloud you have ever seen
This is what my mouth is for
Candles with fresh flames
All flames are fresh
Crisp clean white shirts in washing powder adverts made
from fire

A whistle blows and my blistered hands are reaching for planks and metal helplessly trying to keep myself travelling on the rails of what I have been born into my heart is racing against the clock that it powers fast train noise faster train noise sound of shouting sound of screaming...

I am eating a brand new bread bacon sandwich and have just had a mouthful of tea

War Jelly

The waiters wheel the war jelly into the restaurant of the world
Terrified tanks suspended in the wobble of raspberry
Hardened to dying dining eyes look at the shape and blink
Lips still like statues
A jelly set in the mould of death
Floating dropped rifles
Millions of tiny weightless now silent soldier people
Vertical planes
Engine flames
Yellow and orange to black
Smoke pluming in the chubby glacial red
Permanently on the menu

Fur

My cat looked pale in the face
Or was that her fur?
She was a white cat after all
What was making her look so ill and off-colour?
Then I remembered my cat was black
Wow she must be feeling really poorly to go so white like that
Or maybe her hair had turned white due to worry?
Do cats worry?
Perhaps she had seen a ghost
Then I remembered my cat died last year

ARE YOU THE ORANGUTAN WHO SAYS "YES" ALL THE TIME?

NO.

Thanks

Tom Hanks sits on a bench in a spaceship
Holding a box of chocolates and a DIY spear
He is dying from AIDS
Has a urine infection
And is wearing an animated cartoon cowboy hat
No chocolates in the chocolate box
Just a volleyball with Meg Ryan's face on it
Her face painted with the blood from the Nazis he has killed
On the inside he is a young boy holding a tommy gun
A huge light brown dog stands guard
The spaceship is now a train on the sea
The sea is covered with 3D snow
He is a heroic World War Two special needs cowboy from
Alabama with a massive beard and a toothache who is being
held hostage by Somali pirates
That's his job

Donor

I threw a cricket ball clot of my blood up at the cold sky
Heavy and dark and red
I wanted to donate something to the generous atmosphere
The air gives itself to me every day
Fills me with what I need to stay alive
The sky has colourful blood
My blood type is red
I watched as my thrown ball grew smaller
And then bigger again
Caught what I tried to give with my hand
Hard and sudden with some jagged edges
It hurt like a fast fist
I dropped the round crimson planet of me into my coat pocket
and realised I was bleeding
I had cut myself with my own blood

Weatherman

I've got this friend, Nigel, who works in the sky. He isn't a pilot, air steward, astronaut or a tower crane driver. Nigel works the weather. He took me up to his place of work once and gave me a guided tour of his warehouse full of weather. The first door we came to had the words, BLUE SKY written in black marker pen on the badly painted white door.

I need to get some proper signs made for these doors, he said apologetically.

Nigel opened the door and the room was full of blue sky. At least I think it was a room, there weren't any clouds or corners, and I couldn't see where the walls were or where the room ended. I went to step into the room where the blue sky was kept.

WOAH WOAH WOAH! shouted Nigel, WHAT ARE YOU DOING?

He grabbed me by the arm, pulled me back and closed the door behind him. As I turned around I could see a bright light coming from around the corner. I began to walk towards it. Nigel took out two pairs of Blues Brothers style safety glasses from his top pockets. We put them on and walked round to where the light was coming from. Propped up against the wall were hundreds and thousands of forks of lightning, all resting against each other like old garden tools in a shed. It was a bit of a mess to be honest.

Nigel mate, don't you think you should have a bit of a tidy up, that's expensive stuff that isn't it?

What, fork lightning? No. Not really. I don't use it that often anyway. There's the sheet lightning up there look.

I looked up to see the bright sheets varying in size and thickness sat on a large shelf like books. I could see one was dripping from the corner. A small puddle of lightning had gathered on the floor. I pointed it out to Nigel and he mopped it up with a wooden handled mop that hissed and fizzed as he put it back in the bucket full of water. I couldn't believe that he was the only person that worked up there.

Yeah it's a lot of responsibility, but I used to work on a checkout so this is much more interesting for me. There aren't any customers but I can make people's day. Did you notice how it was sunny on your wedding day and I couldn't make it because I was at work? There you go.

Really? Well why don't you ever give us a white Christmas then dickhead?

I don't know, I just think people might twig that it's man-made weather. There's the rain tanks look, all the different types of rain in there Rob. Heavy, light, torrential.

The rain was falling to the floor of the glass tanks and bouncing back up to the ceiling and back down like some sort of really miserable screen saver.

Look at those raindrops Rob. They are just waiting. This weather is just waiting to be used. The thing is, I get quite attached to it. Look at that cloud over there, I can't let her go because she reminds me of my Mum. This place is full of old tattered weather, stuff I can't bring myself to use. Sometimes it feels like an old people's home in here, but with old weather instead of old people. You know like ninety year old thunder sitting in a chair waiting to die?

Errrr yeah OK Nigel I think I better be getting back now.

Ah but Rob, I haven't shown you where I keep the sunshine yet.

Don't worry mate, I've seen it before.

Brighton Peach

Amongst the multi-coloured sepia TV static stones of
Brighton beach
Sits the dry stone of a peach
There is always one
Resting atop the under stones
Reflecting on its former life as the core of the sun with the
hairy skin
A time spent encompassed in sweet wet sunshine and
vitamin C
Until it was eaten out into this world
And dropped by the ocean
A peach long digested
The sticky fingered peach beach person
Is no longer sticky fingered or a beach person
The stones it rests upon are simply stones
Stones of a beach

Jumping

To jump into a swimming pool full of water is a decision
A decision I make once in a while
When you have an opportunity to jump
How do you know whether it's going to work out for you?
To throw your body and brain into something
Unknowing of the consequences
Like the water of the pool, the time of the future is there
Waiting to be jumped into
So why do I sit at my desk thinking about the future
Instead of trying to jump into it?
You can't jump into the future like you can jump into a
swimming pool
Time travel happens slowly and naturally
One second at a time
1
2
3
I wish I could jump into the future like I can jump into a
swimming pool
If the future was as wet and predictable as that
Would I want to continue living?
What if I jump into the future and can't get out?
I am in the future now compared to where I was when I started
writing this
I am a really slow time traveller
But the speed is just right for me

ARE YOU THE ORANGUTAN WHO SAYS "YES" ALL THE TIME?

NO.

The Safety Of Biscuits

You know Custard Creams? she whispered.
Yes, I whispered.
Not them, she whispered.
You know Jammie Dodgers? she whispered.
Yes, I whispered.
Not them.
You know Rich Teas?
Yes.
Not them.
You know Bourbons?
Yes.
Not them.
You know chocolate Digestives, the ones with the layer of caramel under the chocolate?
Yes.
Not them.
You know those pink wafers that are really light?
Yes.
Not them.
You know those malt ones with the pictures of cows on?
Yes.
Not them.

It was weird because the bank we both worked in was being held up by men with guns.
A scene of complete and utter mayhem.
Sawn-off shotguns, balaclavas, shouting and tears.
We were just sitting there on the floor with our hands cable tied behind our backs having a dysfunctional conversation about her favourite type of biscuit.

Gravel Travel

On my way to the supermarket
I saw a man throwing small stones at a wall

I am throwing these stones into the future, he said to me
without looking as I walked past

I watched them hit the wall of the red brick building and fall to
the pavement
Together, these stones had once been gravel
They were landing far enough apart from each other to return
them to the status of stones

The next day I went to the supermarket again to remember
what I had forgotten
The man was no longer there but the stones were on the floor
He really had thrown them into the future

The Normal Song

I've got a Clubcard and a girlfriend, I'm normal
I've got a toilet and a U-bend, I'm normal
I've got a bath mat and a sieve, I'm normal
I've got a flat where I can live, I'm normal
It's all so normal

I've got a kettle and a toaster, I'm normal
National Insurance number like I'm supposed to, I'm normal
I've got a TV and some channels, I'm normal
I remember Helen Daniels, I'm normal

Normal, Normal, Normal

I'm a rabbit I eat carrots, I'm normal
I'm a rabbit in a cage, I'm normal
I'm a rabbit on a plate, I'm normal
How did it all get so normal?

I play football and get paid, it's normal
I play football and don't get paid, it's normal
I pay to watch football, it's normal
Is this really quite so normal?

I've got two eyes and a nose and so does a dog
I've got two ears and a tongue and so does a dog
I drink water and I sleep and so does a dog
But NO humans are nothing like dogs

A little girl goes missing, it's on the news
A man is arrested, it's on the news
People they are searching, it's on the news
Then suddenly it's not on the news

I am topless next to murder, I'm on page 3
I am topless next to famine, look at me
Breasts, sport, murder, celebrity
Is that normal or absurdity?

It's become normal that guns and bombs exist
We must really need them
Is there something I missed?
People wouldn't build things to kill, would they?
That would be absurd in every way
It's not absurd, it's normal

A small group of people run the country
They are much more clever than you and me
It's their job to make sure that we are all OK
I don't think we are OK

I'm going to do the best I can before I die
To try and understand the reason why
Things got out of hand, so long ago
Can I do it?
I don't know

Bar Of Brain

When I was born my brain was as hard and fresh as soap is
when you first take it from the packet
Definite shape and lines
My mind has been sitting in a soap dish with accidental water
for years
The edges now soft and near translucent from life coming in
through the sense holes
I know there is still some brain in there that is untouched
It is solid and stubborn in the middle
Pure and without footprints
Nobody can get to it
Not even me

Outside World

Walking through Leicester in the morning, there were houses right next to the pavement. Do you know what I mean? Right next to the pavement. I heard someone knocking on a door from inside one of the houses. I went to the doorstep and said, Hello?

Hello, sorry to bother you, but can I come in? asked a voice from inside the house.

Come in? It's not really mine, I don't own the outside, I replied.

Well whose is it then? Who owns it?

I don't know, we kind of share it I guess.

Oh that sounds nice, if I come in can you show me around? Give me a tour?

What? Show you around the world? Give you a world tour?

Yes.

No I'm sorry I've got a train to catch.

IT'S THE WIND'S BIRTHDAY TODAY, TAKE ITS CAKE OUTSIDE AND WATCH IT BLOW OUT THE CANDLES.

Balloons Full Of Pop

It's February 21st again
The curtains are as closed as they will close
Ballooned corners of front room continue to bulge
Filled with air of New Year's Eve party preparation
Apart from the green ones that have gone down
Unlike lead balloons
The cheeks went from their colour
Slowly deflating from GREEN to green
The final sober breaths of 2012
Contained in multi-coloured time capsules
Time capsules with thin skins
A month and twenty one days have passed
The time has come to pop the party
Balloon by balloon

I take the pin from the nearest badge
It is in my bedroom
A tiny bayonet that gives my finger more of a point
Prick goes the bayonet
Pop goes the balloon
If only war was as easy to burst

Invisible memories of 2012 spill into the air of the newish year
I brace myself for some sort of time clash chemical reaction
And nothing happens

Things Are

How are things?

Yeah OK thanks. Oh hold on, which things?

I don't know, the usual things.

Usual things such as ice cube trays?

Yes they are usual things.

My ice cube tray is OK.

Yeah I think that, not about yours but about mine.

I think they are OK, they work don't they?

Depends what you are using them for, they are particularly good for making ice cubes.

I don't really like cold drinks.

How are things though?

I don't know how things are, but they are.

Things are.

They really are aren't they? Things are.

How did things come to be things?

I don't know they just did, we let things become a thing.

So that we can ask, how are things?

Nature

I was watching the television with the window open at night when a small bat flew into the room. It flew around for a short time and settled on the arm of the sofa that I was lying on. The arm of the sofa nearest to my head and furthest from my feet. The bat faced the television. I guess you could say we were watching television together. I thought bats were meant to be blind. I slowly got up from the sofa and kneeled down to have a look at the bat. It looked so relaxed. Completely at ease with being a bat. It was as if the bat knew what it was in my living room for. It knew why it was there more than I did to be honest. Within five minutes of it being there the bat had made the house her own. I felt like I was the visitor and I had just disturbed the bat and he had welcomed me into her home. Was the bat male or female? I didn't know and I wasn't going to try to check. I told myself that I was the alpha male in this situation. I had been kneeling and looking at the bat for a while now. It kept trying to look around me to get a better view of the television but I wanted to look at the bat in the face. The bat was better than TV. Even if there had been a documentary about bats on the television, I had the HD pay-per-view fibre optic bat right in front of me. The bat's face was about a centimetre square. It was a very concentrated area of the world. There was a huge amount of face in that small area. Eyes, a nose, a mouth, a bit of skin to make up the cheeks. Creases and folds making shadows and lighter bits. It looked like the face of a hyena that looked a bit like a pot-bellied pig. I walked through into the kitchen to make a cup of tea and poured a bit of milk onto a plate for the bat. I don't know why I thought the bat would like the milk. I remembered giving a hedgehog some milk on a plate when I was little and this kind of felt like a similar situation to that. Magical but firmly rooted in nature, like a really good sunset. I have probably seen more bats in my lifetime than hedgehogs but I keep them next to each other in my brain. They live in a room that I don't open too often. Also in that room are birds' nests that I saw in hedges when I was little that had blue eggs in them. I think that's all that's in there, it's not a big room, but it's one I like.

I poured the milk onto the plate, white on white, and walked back through into the living room to find that the bat had gone. I felt like saying something like hello to see if it was there, but I stayed silent. I looked down at the plate of milk and didn't know what to do with it. I hate wasting milk but I knew it was going to be difficult to pour the milk from the plate back into the milk bottle. If I cling filmed it then that would be the first time I had ever cling filmed milk. I do love new experiences. If I did keep it I knew that when I went to put it on my breakfast in the morning I would think, oh some of this milk that is on my cereal was meant for a bat. I put the cup of tea on the coffee table and quickly poured the milk into the tea. Why did coffee get a table and tea didn't? I bet over the course of history there have been as many, if not more, cups of tea put on coffee tables as cups of coffee. The tea with the milk in that was for the bat was now a write-off but I still drank it. I had taken one for the bat.

I wondered if the bat was happy flying around the skies of London. Pigeons, bats and aeroplanes were the three things that shared my local sky. I have never seen a pigeon and a bat flying at the same time. I would like that. Bats are so close to being black birds. Teeth instead of beaks. They have very different flying techniques to pigeons. Pigeons don't really flutter. If the colour grey could fly I think it would fly like a pigeon. I sat down on the sofa and realised that the film I had been watching had finished. The news was on. I looked at the colours of the studio. I often have to stop myself from everything just being colours. Life is much simpler if everything is just colours. I looked at the red bits of the studio and the gradient of the light on the walls. The newsreader was kind of pink. A cross between pink and white I guess. She had red lips and squarish bits of white in her mouth. Her hair was yellow with brown in it. She had a face with eyes in it and she was using them to look at the camera. It was Sunday night. I have never been able to shake the feeling that school had planted in me for Sunday nights. I had been working in an art supplies shop as a retail assistant for the past three years after being made redundant from my job as an art director for an advertising agency. My shift started at 9.15 am the next day and I was due to finish my shift at 6.30pm.

I would have my lunch from 1-2pm and have a fifteen minute break at 4.30pm. I kind of knew what to expect from tomorrow. I wasn't excited about tomorrow. Looking at the TV that had turned black after switching it off, I began to think that it was not such a good thing that I wasn't excited about tomorrow. I should always be excited about tomorrow. Even if tomorrow is due to be the worst day I should still be excited about just how bad it is going to be. How bad is tomorrow going to be? Tomorrow is going to be really bad. Oh FANTASTIC! I can't wait to see just how bad it is going to be. Like an awful film. I love watching awful films. Can I pretend that my life is an awful film? Why would I want to do that? Why not pretend it is a good film? Why not just try to have an exciting life? It is within my power to make that happen. I looked at the blank screen and then at my watch. It was 12.31am. It was time for bed but I wasn't ready for bed. For the first time in a while I didn't feel like the day was over. I stood up and looked outside, it was predictably dark and it was raining. Before I had been able to stop myself I was walking down the street where I live. The rain was making me and my clothes wet, but not enough to make me want an umbrella or to stop walking. Sometimes rain is my favourite type of weather. Especially rain at night. I like all the weather really. If I could pick one type of weather to have on permanently it would probably be sunny, but not too hot, with a few decent shaped clouds in the sky so there is something to look at. That would be my daytime. At nighttime I would want to be able to see the shiny bits of sky. Again I would want a few clouds up there as clouds can enhance the moon sometimes. The veil at the marriage of beauty and night. If I could have my perfect weather all the time, it wouldn't take me long to miss the others. Weather is like a group of mates to me. Frosty mornings, overcast afternoons, I like to see them every now and again. Snow, rain, bright, dark, wind, breeze, sun, moon. Maybe a life partner is all the weathers at once that you can live with. Weather is good company when I am alone.

Walking through London at that time on a Sunday night/ Monday morning, you still have to press the button at the pedestrian crossing to cross the road. Chicken shops are warm with fried chicken coals. I couldn't remember the last time I just went out for a walk. This was the first time I had done it on a Sunday that was now a Monday. I walked and the further I walked the better it felt. After sitting inside for most of the weekend I was cross at myself for not doing this earlier. I wanted to walk, but I didn't want to walk far, as I knew I was going to have to walk back the way I came. Nothing really happened on the walk. I had my good new shoes on and I thought about them quite a lot. I had spent a bit more money on a really solid pair of shoes with some birthday money I had been given. My parents had paid for these shoes. I was dressed in clothes my parents had bought me. A thick coat, a thick jumper. I think I may have bought the trousers myself. I felt like I was equipped for something in those clothes. Soft but effective armour for the constant yet absent battle called life.

It was raining, my shoes were wet but my feet were dry. I thought I might have seen a fox but they must have been somewhere else. It looked like exactly the right kind of light for foxes. Street light. Where were all the pigeons? Do all the pigeons that live in London have nests? Do they stay near their families? Every pigeon, a father, a son, a daughter, a mother. Is there an average time when a pigeon goes to sleep? 9.13pm? Do they ever find it hard to sleep?

When I got home I saw that the living room light was on. Had I left it on? I couldn't remember leaving it on. I got my keys out of my pocket, opened the door and went upstairs to the flat. I went through into the living room and it was as I had left it. I turned the light off, poured myself a glass of water and went to bed. My bedroom is big enough for a bed, some drawers, a bookcase and two wardrobes. The reason I have two wardrobes is because in my last flat the bedroom didn't come with a wardrobe and the lady who was moving out said I could buy her wardrobe for forty pounds. So when it came time to leave I couldn't leave the wardrobe that was now mine. I had never owned my own wardrobe before. So now I've got two wardrobes in my bedroom, one with clothes in it and one filled with things I haven't thrown away. It is an ugly scene in that wardrobe. If someone from the

Fung Shui department came round and assessed my wardrobe situation I think they would start crying. Having something in your room that you never want to open cannot be good for your mental health. It is a wooden cloud that rains splinters into my eyes every time I look at it.

My bedroom is quite a cold place because the window doesn't shut properly. I tried to fill the gap with wire wool last year but the cold turned it to rust. Grey hair that went ginger. Wire wool had been in my good books for a while after keeping the mice out of my life. It is harder to keep the cold out than it is to keep the mice out. The cold is bigger and more aggressive.

I am quite a tall person, about 6 foot 2 I think I was the last time my Mum put a pencil on the top of my head. Those marks have been painted over now. Because I am tall my feet stick out of the end of my duvet, that was until recently when I had the idea to unzip my sleeping bag and tuck it into the end of my bed creating an overlap of cover and warmth. This has been one of the best things I have done in my life. I put my feet to the end of my bed and turned off my bedside lamp. I then turned my lamp back on and set my alarm on my digital watch for 7.15 am. I was going to bed on Monday morning. This was my favourite part of Monday morning. I had done this before. Sleeping. Sleeping was something that nobody had taught me. I could do it pretty much as soon as I was born. I was probably asleep in the womb before I was fully formed. I slept as my body developed over a nine month period. WOW I'M SLEEPING AND MY EYES ARE BEING MADE, BY ME. I was really nailing life back then. Working really hard to get some fingers and wrists and a heart and some lungs. How did I know what to do? When did my heart beat for the first time? Was it the minute sperm hit egg? The moment I was conceived was I going for it? Or was it a gradual process? It's not beating, it's beating a bit, it's beating all the time now. That first nine months I did something incredible without even trying. Went from a nobody to a somebody. Probably the busiest nine months of my life, growing all those limbs and organs. That night I slept quite well. I very rarely have dreams that I remember. Martin Luther King of dreams is safe for now.

My alarm went off on my watch. I never give myself much time in the morning. It is a quick operation. I get up as quickly as I can. I pretend I am a tent and it's about to rain. If I can be bothered to pretend that is. Sometimes it takes too much effort and I don't have the drive. My morning routine is simple. I get out of bed, I take my towel off the radiator that is never switched on, walk to the bathroom, click down the red switch that is outside the bathroom that powers the shower, walk into the bathroom, pull the light cord if I need to, turn the shower onto the red setting, get in the shower and get myself as wet as I possibly can with the water that is available to me. About three years ago I started using a brand of soap and the first time I used it I knew I was going to use it for as long as the company kept producing it and as long as I could afford it. Not that it is expensive but I try to keep a certain amount of fear in me to keep myself from becoming complacent. I use this soap and it makes me clean. That is what I want from soap. I make sure I really wash myself because I went through a stage when I was a teenager of just standing under the shower and not doing anything. I kept this up until my sister told my Mum and Dad that I really smelt of B.O. I don't know why my sister noticed and my parents didn't, I guess it was because I didn't wrestle against my parents on a regular basis. They were, after all, a tag team. After it was brought to my parents' attention that I had moved to Smelltown and had recently become the mayor of said town, I received such a telling off it made me want to be clean for the rest of my life. If I have a bad gig I make sure that after it I really wash myself really hard to try and get it off me. Behind my ears, especially in my ears, wash out the silence of the audience.

When I get out of the shower I dry myself and then go into my bedroom and I put my clothes on. I don't like getting dressed. I've still got that thing that I had as a child, I hate getting dressed. I also don't like going to bed. Now that I no longer live with my parents I am always naked and never asleep. I don't have that many clothes, I don't want to waste time choosing. Once I am dressed I have a cup of tea and some cereal. I recently started mixing muesli with Corn Flakes and I'm not sure if I will be able to go back to just Corn Flakes or just muesli. I have tasted the crunch of paradise on the end of a spoon. When my cereal bowl is empty again, I clean my teeth and put the things in my pockets that we all need and leave the house with a coat on if I need one. If you leave the house with empty pockets there is only so far you can go for so long.

I normally get the underground train to work on a morning. There is still a glimmer of excitement in being underground and on a train. The thought of somebody saying, OK we are going to put trains underground, must have sounded like what insanity sounds like. The ground is so full of ground. I wonder what it was like the day they started. A single man with a shovel digging into the London mud shouting, THIS IS WHERE THE STAIRS ARE GOING TO BE. LOOK AT ME EVERYBODY. I'M DIGGING OUT THE STAIRS. The job in front of those people was a big one. Unknowing if the ground above them was going to hold up. I don't know what machines they would have used but I do know that the ground under London used to be full of earth and mud and now it is full of miserable commuters. Hey come on guys, we are on a train underground! Digging out the Victoria line, where did they put all that earth that they took from the tunnels and stations? Was it used to make hills? Or were they scattered over Great Britain? The ashes of car journeys to and from work in the capital.

The tube I took that morning was full of people and silence. Ladies putting their makeup on in tiny mirrors as if they were getting ready for a party they didn't want to go to. I started to think about that bat. What was it doing in my living room? Bats are a creature I have always felt a strong affinity with. I am quite positive I am not Batman though. I don't do Batman type things, like live in Gotham City or have a butler. My name is not Clark. I have always had Clarks shoes though. Oh no, Clark Kent is Superman not Batman. Bruce Wayne! One of the chosen few with two first names. Fiona Bruce is another one. Steve Bruce. I used to think Fiona Bruce and Steve Bruce were married. I saw Fiona Bruce reading the newspaper on the tube once and I thought, oh that must sound great in her head.

I realised I had been staring at the lady opposite straight in the eyes for the past five minutes. My eyes had been open but they had not been looking. I looked down at my feet. Clarks shoes. I knew they were not Superman's shoes. Maybe he wore shoes like this when he was working as a journalist but not when he was dressed as a superhero. A hero that is super. Oh that hero is just super. Superman. Supertramp. Every now and again band names unveil themselves to me. Suddenly they make sense. Daft Punk. Punk that is daft. The Happy Mondays. Super Furry Animals. Talking Heads. The Coral. Names of things pass me by sometimes. The next station is Oxford Circus. I picked up my bag from by my feet. It was a light rucksack. It contained a book that I had forgotten to read again and a bottle of water that I hadn't drunk from yet. The walk to the art shop was uneventful that morning, as it had been almost every time I had walked it. I am OK with that. I don't want events to take place at that time in the morning, apart from the event of me getting given something for free from a company who are doing a promotion. I remember one beautiful morning outside Oxford Circus station when Lurpak were giving out free croissants with tiny packs of Lurpak (just enough though) and a plastic knife. The best things in life are true. Is that right? No, it's the best things in life are free isn't it? I've had some pretty good times with Lurpak that I have paid for to be honest. Sometimes juice brands give out bottles of juice for free. Some people think Tesco give their stuff away for free. Those people are thieves. I have got a real thing about getting stuff for free. I like it.

I started work at 9.15am. I had a lunch break at 1pm for an hour. I had a break at 4.30pm for fifteen minutes. I finished work at 6.30pm.

When I finished work it was dark outside. I walked back to the underground station the same way I came. The pavement wasn't wet because it hadn't been raining or been cleaned. People don't give out free croissants on an evening. They give out free papers. The tube is always very busy on a night. The platform packed with people, most of them thinking about their dinner. Trains come into the platforms quickly and every so often someone who isn't thinking about their dinner makes the most of that fact. There is no service between Oxford Circus and Seven Sisters station due to a passenger under a train at Euston. If you are under a train can you still be a passenger? When I hear these announcements death gets me in a headlock for a few minutes. That decision to end yourself. To press stop and eject yourself from the DVD player of life. I know a man who took his own life. He took it. He took it away from us. As if to say, It's mine, you can't have it anymore. I don't want to show it to you. I remember the night the police were in my flat. When they left I put a Flaming Lips live concert DVD on. The people in the crowd all dressed in fancy dress. Hands in the air. Fists clenched gripping at life. They looked so alive. When death gets close it seems to inflate life. Like sometimes when you try to pop a bubble in a piece of bubble wrap and the bubble doesn't pop, the air just moves into the next bubble making it more full.

The train pulled into the platform and I just managed to get on. The front of my head was very close to the back of a lady's head. If I had held my camera phone up to take a picture, her hair would have filled the screen. I don't know how many people were on that tube but the people with seats were rich. Rich with relaxation. People were touching each other in the least sexual way known to man. An arm against an arm. An arse against a thigh. All contact but no touch. An intimate experience without the intimacy. Packed like sardines, if sardines could stand up and be miserable and tired and going home from work. Some people on that train however, were definitely not going home. Some people were going out. Out on a weeknight. It was a Monday night and some people in England were about to have the best night of their lives. Some will go out on a date and fall in love. Babies will be born and people will die and some people who have never met will cook the exact same meal in completely different kitchens. Will they? Same brand of sausages, same brand of potato, same brand broccoli, same brand gravy. Will they? Does that happen? Or is every home cooked meal in Britain ever so slightly different? The train pulled into Walthamstow Central. I had to get some food from the supermarket. The days of the trolley were over for me. I got what I needed from the supermarket. I barely looked. It was one of those. It was dark again. I put my key in the door and made my way upstairs. Walking through into the kitchen I knew what was ahead of me for the evening. Cook food, eat food, watch something, go to bed. I put my new belongings in the fridge and walked through into the living room. I switched on the light and began to walk over to switch the television on. I took a step and then stopped. I stopped. I made some sort of noise. Not a scream or a shout but something like that. A noise that you make when you see something that you are not expecting. Sat on the coffee table facing the door was the bat from last night. It looked at me like it had been waiting for me to get home. Not only was there a bat, but there was also a hedgehog. The hedgehog had its back to me. It was facing the television.

Water

Water is the smell of a pint of orange cordial
Before you've added the cordial
Similar in taste to the broken pelvis of a melted snowman
The backbone of a snowflake
The unsalted tear of a poodle
The elbow of a puddle

Clear science that allows me to live
No wonder I get so cross when I spill it

Christmas Snow Melting
In The Beard Of Jesus Christ

The Christmas decorations in the sky are really nice aren't they?

What do you mean? The stars?

Yes.

Well they are up all year round.

Yes but they look so nice at Christmas, they are all CHRISTMASSY. Like Jesus or a snowman.

Or Jesus in the shape of a snowman?

No not fat Jesus. A snowman made from wood. The good thing about a snowman made from wood is that it never melts. I tried banging nails into snow and lost my hammer. You can set fire to a wooden snowman when you've finished with it. This will not only keep you warm but will also melt all the other snowmen in the surrounding area. So keep in mind the more facial features and buttons of coal you give him the more substantial amount of time he will burn for. So elaborate with facial expressions at Christmas.

I HAD A FLATMATE
CALLED KEVIN
WHO LIVED
IN A SHELL

I GUESS THAT MEANS
THAT I DID AS WELL

Cup Of Tea

That's my cup of tea.

No that's not your cup of tea, that's my cup of tea.

No, I mean that's my cup of tea, a cup of tea is my cup of tea.

Well that particular cup of tea is not your cup of tea, that particular cup of tea is my cup of tea. To claim every cup of tea is your cup of tea is quite ridiculous. You don't own every cup of tea, not every cup of tea is your cup of tea. Don't you remember when you told me that you don't care for peppermint tea?

Oh no, peppermint tea is not my cup of tea.

Well peppermint tea is my cup of tea, it's my bag.

Your teabag?

No. Peppermint tea is my bag, it's not my tea bag, it's my cup of tea.

Sink

A swan decorates a canal
A white blouse over its feathers
What is it wearing that for?
An insecure swan?
Strange to see a swan far from one hundred percent
happy with its own reflection
No floating in the delight of the hand it was dealt
Bags clumsily underlining world beaten eyes
It looks like it will sink if it stops kicking
Slowly quicksand sinking into the dark of the unbottled
The orange of its beak disappearing under
Slow float like

Yellow Supermarket

Take a melon from the shelf take a melon for yourself
Take a lemon from the shelf take a lemon for yourself
Put the lemon and the melon in a trolley for yourself
Take bananas from the shelf take bananas for yourself
Tin of sweetcorn from the shelf tin of sweetcorn for yourself
Ignore the fact that there's a green giant on the tin
He may be green and he may also be a giant but he would be
nothing without the sweetcorn
Yellow peppers from the shelf in a trolley for yourself
Take a grapefruit from the shelf take a grapefruit for yourself
Grapefruit sounds like great fruit, that's because that is
what it is
Why is a grapefruit called a grapefruit? There is already a fruit
called a grape
And a grapefruit looks nothing like the grape that's a fruit

Take a pineapple from the shelf take a pineapple for yourself
It may look brown and green on the outside
But fruit is just like humans
It's what's on the inside that counts
Not in the case of the pink grapefruit

The bottom of your trolley's getting yellow
The bottom of your trolley's getting yellow
Lower your chin down to your shopping and think of each
product as a buttercup
IS YOUR CHIN YELLOW? Do you like SHOPPING?
You can't see because mirrors are quite rare in supermarkets

Don't take an apple from the shelf don't take an apple
for yourself
Not even golden delicious
Don't be fooled into thinking they are yellow by the name
They are golden by the name and gold is not the same

Move from fruit and veg down to dairy it is where you'll find
the cheese

So much yellow in the cheese so much yellow you're so pleased
Take some Cheddar from the shelf
Take some Edam from the shelf
Take some Stilton from the shelf
Take some Stilton for yourself
Take away the Stilton it has green contained in it

Margarine and butter from the shelf for yourself
Yellow jumping out at you from shelf to yourself
You start to run down the aisles grabbing all that shines
Grab some Marmite for the lid
Grab some Marmite you just did, eat the lid
Yellow plastic in your teeth yellow plastic in your teeth
Yellow plastic in your teeth this does mean that you're a thief
A voice comes over the tannoy system
Security please go to the cereal aisle where a man is attempting
to make a fort out of Shredded Wheat boxes, lemon fresh
Domestos bottles and pineapple chunks

I am in my fort they cannot get me
I have got supplies for one year maybe three
Peanut M&Ms, Jelly Tots, lemon puffs
Orangina, lemon tarts, barley water, rubber gloves

The security staff knock down my fort
I sit surrounded in colour

Why Yellow?

Yellow because I don't want to live my life in the dark
I don't want to live in the shadow of death
I want to live on the bright side
ON FULL BEAM WITH CAPS LOCK ON
I want to stand and to stand for standing up
To try to do good and to be a good person
To shine away from politics and war and all the other important
things I don't understand
That I know for a fact we as a species have made up
Someone drew the letter O for the first time
It just caught on and it wasn't that long ago
I look at politicians and cannot relate to them in any way
I know they have faces and hands and fingers with fingernails
and I know that they need to eat and to sleep and to feed
their families
Sometimes it feels like the world is a pub quiz and I am sat at a
table on my own and I don't know any of the answers
But I look to the sun and feel the warmth on my face and am
certain that this is something real that humans have always
done and always will do no matter how absurd this planet gets

Yellow hope

Yellow to me is the light that isn't at the end of the tunnel
It's the light that surrounds us
It's a poached or scrambled or fried egg on a Saturday morning
If that egg was grey instead of yellow
Would the experience be as magical?
Grey scrambled egg served on a bed of death
That's what I'm fighting against

Number Plate

I saw a man screwing a number plate into the ground at the base of Mount Everest. When I inquired into his activity he looked up at me and began to speak.

The Earth is travelling through space, we need a number plate don't we?

Why are you putting it here? I replied.

Because this is the front of the Earth, Mount Everest is the nose piercing through space.

Are you sure the number plate isn't a bit small?

No it is just right.

Are you sure this is the front of the world?

No, this is the front of the Earth, not the front of the world. The Earth and the world are two very different things.

So what is the front of the world?

My wife's face.

Big Red Book

I am approached by an elderly man who I half recognise from the television. He is holding a large red book. The man shakes me by the hand and I am driven to a television studio and given a seat on a sofa on a stage in front of a large studio audience who are seated again after giving me a standing ovation. The man with the book goes on to read incorrect facts about me and my life.

You were born in Bangkok to your loving parents Dean and Margaret.

Dean and Margaret then appear and sit next to me on the sofa. They look at me with the expression you use to look at somebody who you don't know but you are pretending to recognise. Over the next hour a range of friends and work colleagues from schools I didn't go to and jobs I didn't do are introduced onto the stage. The man then hands me the book and says, Rob Auton this isn't your life.

I know it isn't, I reply.

BUT WHAT IS YOUR LIFE? he shouts with the studio disappearing into total darkness bar a white-hot spotlight on me.

I don't know, but it's not this.

From the black the voice says, I'm waiting for you to do something with your life so I can give you a book and say, Rob Auton, this is your life.

Look mate, I say, this is my life enough without somebody else telling me what my life is. Like when I get Clubcard vouchers through the post and I get excited and then realise what I am excited about. I shut my eyes and tell myself, this is my life. Or when I buy a tin of ten pineapple rings to use two rings to go with some gammon, and I am left with eight pineapple rings in a bowl in the fridge covered in cling film because I only recently learnt that you shouldn't keep tins in the fridge unless you want to die. Then I get worried about whether I am going to eat the pineapple rings before they go off, but I don't just want to eat them on their own because that would be a waste and I don't want to leave them to go off because I know that the hungry child from the TV advert with the phone number across his neck will pop into my head as soon as the pineapple rings rest in the black hole for rubbish and then I sit on my kitchen floor crying saying to myself, this is my life, this is my life.

Can you turn the lights back on please? I ask the darkness. Right, I've got a bone to pick with this programme anyway. Why is it only celebrities and dream lives that you get on This Is Your Life? Why don't you try to raise awareness about things such as homelessness or drug addiction or prostitution? Go into a homeless shelter or a prison and speak to some of the people and find out how they got into their situation and locate all the people that helped them get to where they are. This is your Dad who beat you as a child. This is your teacher who excluded you instead of trying to help you, and this is the person who introduced you to heroin. Real people's lives. Why don't you do that? Instead of making out like people have dream lives and everything is just perfect in their lives because it won't be. You are giving people something false to dream about and work towards.

The studio lights go back up and the audience, the presenter and all of my supposed family and friends have left. There is a man sweeping the floor, I ask him how to get out and he points to a fire exit sign.

ARE YOU THE ORANGUTAN WHO SAYS "YES" ALL THE TIME?

NO.

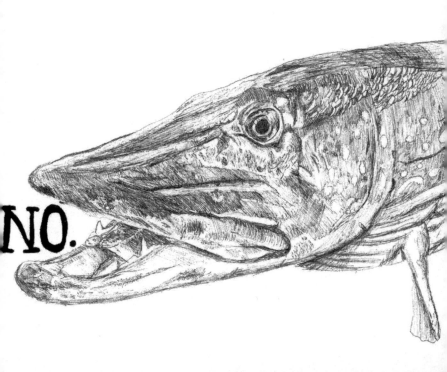

Thirties

In a few years time we will be living in the thirties again
I can imagine thirties Britain now
Countryside, cities, rubbish bins
Some people wearing hats
Others driving cars that might break down
Dogs and cats kept as pets
People falling in love and females having babies
Bits of grass
Glasses of water
Stones with rain on them
We will be able to go to thirties fancy dress parties in our
regular clothes
I hope I live to see the sixties
With the sky and the sea and the summer of sixty nine

Living Creatures

There are two of us standing here
Standing here on the pavement in Edinburgh
Me and a seagull
Oh, the seagull has just flown off
There is one of us standing here on the pavement in Edinburgh
Oh hold on, there are two of us again
Now there are three of us
Fantastic
I wonder if they like me?
Whether the seagulls like me or not, I am part of this group
and together we are three
A man has just arrived with a closed bag of white sliced bread
There are four of us standing here on the pavement in
Edinburgh
Me, two seagulls and a man with a closed bag of white
sliced bread
The closed bag of white sliced bread is now open
The white sliced bread from the bag of white sliced bread is
being thrown onto the pavement
I cannot count how many of us there are now
Layer upon layer of bird and bread
Wing on wing
Sound on sound
Beak on beak
An alive seagull and white sliced bread lasagne
The white sliced bread has been eaten and taken up into the air
in stomachs
There is one of us standing here
Standing here on the pavement in Edinburgh

Kite

The man in the purple jacket stands at the top of the green hill.
He holds onto a piece of string that goes right up into the clouds.
Where's your kite gone?
Arms and fingers move until he is pointing at the sky.
Up there look, there it is.
I look up until clouds.
The sky is my kite.
Hand winds string around fingers.
Round and wind and round and wind.
Sky gets closer.
Rain has less room to fall.
Aeroplane gets louder.
Repeating the winding motion.
Until he winds up his smile.
I begin to feel cold, claustrophobic and intimidated.
Stop.
He listens.
He unwinds.
The sky returns to its original position.

Horse

The horse in the field looked just like a photograph
A photograph of a horse in a field
The horse wasn't as still as a horse in a photograph though
Neither was the field
They were both moving slightly
Not a lot, but just enough to let you know it was real life and
not a photograph
I guess it looked like a few photographs of a horse in a field
Or maybe a film of a horse in a field

Packets Of Light

What do I need for dinner? Pasta. Which shape? It all tastes the same but it is the look of the pasta isn't it? Some shapes are superior skeletons for sauce aren't they? First choice fusilli. As I reached for the flour-sized bag of pasta the supermarket lights went out. Small sounds of surprise and self-censored screams blipped from fellow shoppers. Someone had pressed the supermarket switch from on to off. With my hand raised to the pasta shelf I could no longer see my future dinner. Waving fingers across eyes, I could feel their fan but nothing moved. Just black. Had I been blindfolded by a rival supermarket? I knew that nobody else was moving. We stood frozen and preserved in the temperatureless black ice of the dark.

BING BONG. Good evening shoppers, this is Kevin your store manager speaking. We appear to have temporarily lost our lighting system and the automatic doors have locked. The checkouts are still working so please continue to shop as best you can as we work to fix the problem.

I looked in the direction of where I remembered the checkouts to be and mouthed the word WHAT? With my hand on the pasta I began to question if it was still fusilli. I slowly lowered my empty basket to the ground and began to feel with both hands, trying to get a grip of the interior shapes. Is that a spiral? With the plastic filling in the twirls it could be penne. Penne wouldn't be a disaster. I took it from the shelf and put it blindly into my basket. I could hear rustling from the next aisle. Someone was trying to differentiate the flavours of the crisps by feeling the packets. Good luck. I wasn't going to be venturing down that aisle in a hurry. As my eyes adjusted to the dark it didn't get any lighter. A female voice came from what seemed to be the other end of the supermarket.

Can anybody tell me where the pasta is?

I paused for a second, I hadn't shouted in the supermarket since I lost my Mum every time I went in as a child.

I'M AT THE PASTA. OVER HERE!

OK. Keep shouting pasta and I will try to make my way to you. She said it as if this had happened to her every time she had been shopping.

PASTA PASTA PASTA PASTA, I shouted. Pasta sounds as boring as it tastes before you add anything to it. TASTY PASTA, REALLY TASTY PASTA. Why was I trying to get all the people in the supermarket to eat pasta?

I heard the sound of cautious footsteps coming toward me. Where is the pasta? asked the old far off accent.

It's here, I said, as I patted the black pasta.

But how do you tell which is which?

You have to feel your way to your shape, I told him.

Where's the pasta again? shouted the female voice, and with that came a huge crash of glass and a shriek.

I FOUND THE WINE EVERYBODY.

People were beginning to embrace the absurdity of the situation. We were liberated by the fact that we were shopping, and we were in the dark. It felt like we were at a fancy dress party and the theme was not being able to see in a supermarket. The person who was feeling the crisps was no longer feeling them but freely opening the bags and tasting the flavours. I heard a crunch and then a bag hit the basket, or trolley. The elderly voice was mumbling names of pasta as he felt the shapes.

I slowly moved from the spot I had been fixed to and felt my way along the shelves to where plastic turned to glass and pasta turned to pasta sauce. I took the first jar from the shelf and thought about how much time I had spent deliberating over which sauce to get. I took the jar and smelt it. It smelt of jar.

Confident footsteps strode down the neighbouring aisle.Who brings night vision goggles to a supermarket? Around the corner came footsteps, along with the light from a mobile phone. Oh yes, good idea.

If it rings, I am not answering it, it is a light now, not a phone, and nobody needs a light that rings.

I felt for my phone. Wallet, keys, no phone. With her light pointing in my direction she saw my phoneless hands.

You can follow me if you like? It just means we will have to buy similar things, and I am quite a fussy eater. Do you like bread? I don't like bread, we are not going near the bread. I've eaten bread all my life. Thirty three years of eating bread, my mind tells me bread is OK, but no, I don't want it anymore.

Can you show me where the candles are? I asked. She was still breathing heavily after thinking about bread. I picked up my basket and we began our rubbish safari to the candles.

Movingthrough the aisles we saw other people using their phones to illuminate the shelves. We said hello, and didn't talk about the massive black elephant that was sitting on the supermarket. She guided me past the bin bags, I wondered what button she was pressing to keep her phone lit up. Maybe she was writing a very long text message just using one letter? If it was x and she was in love she might be able to use the text message at the end of her shopping. I looked at her phone to see she had a photograph of a sunflower on her screen, she tapped it to keep it alive, her thumb both the sun and the rain. The vague yellow light reflected on the bin bags. Orange boxes of matches came into view, then large packets of table candles.

I took a pack of candles and a box of matches. The lady held the sunflower phone over the box as I struck. I have always liked the smell of the sandpaper on the side when the strip has been used a few times. I wish I had been there at the moment when the idea to put sandpaper on the side of a box of matches was born. The match tore into brief sound as I struck. The light it gave off extinguished the flame of the sunflower. The whole section now romantically lit. Brillo pads, washing up gloves, dusters. It felt like we had won a candlelit shopping experience for two in the supermarket of our choice.

Fellow shoppers arrived from the surrounding aisles, moths carrying baskets, faces glowing in the dark.

BING BONG. OK everybody, Kevin your store manager here again. I have just come off the phone to the technician and he will not be with us for at least two hours. I am very sorry for the inconvenience. I started this supermarket fourteen years ago, this has never happened before. It is normally empty when the lights are off. Tonight has been a special experience for me. I love this supermarket, I love how hard and level the floor is and I love how badly lit it is when the lights are on. The tubs. The tins. The cartons. The cans. The beeps. The bags. I have always dreamt of this supermarket as a party venue. This is the closest to a party it has ever got in here. We have all the food and drink you could ask for but supermarkets are not where parties happen. I wish we could all go to the drinks aisle and celebrate being alive like in the original draft of this story but some changes had to be made. I'm sorry.

With that the lights in the supermarket blinked back to full. The automatic doors powered open. Our candles burnt redundant flames. People held their hands over their eyes until they could look again. When we adjusted to what we were used to, we looked at each other as if we had tasted what it could be like.

"Holiday"

I'm on "holiday" in Inverted Commas.

Oh that sounds nice, is it "hot" in Inverted Commas?

Yes it is "hot" in Inverted Commas.

Is it "busy" in Inverted Commas?

Yes there are lots of "people" in Inverted Commas. It's "nice" in Inverted Commas but you don't really feel like you are ever on "holiday" in Inverted Commas.

How long are you going to "be" in Inverted Commas for?

Why? Does it "annoy" you that I'm in Inverted Commas?

No you can stay there if you "like it" in Inverted Commas.

Socks

Dark is the palette of my sock drawer
I open it and bats fly out
All that's missing is a moon and a werewolf howling at it
I could pick a sock at random
Tie it around my arm
Pay my respects to the dead
My sock puppets are dressed for a funeral
They cry dark cotton tears
Magpies without the white bits
Humbugs without the stripes
Badgers covered in coal

Death Is My Mr Motivator

He stands in a brightly lit TV studio on a black gym mat
Located at the bottom of my mind
Somewhere near the back of my tongue

Clad in bone tight black Lycra
His scythe leans up against the white studio wall

He performs out of time star jumps to the music I will have
played at my funeral
Encourages me to make the most of my time on Earth
Write it down!
Say it out loud!
See how it goes!
Work on it!

Death never tires
He makes the Energiser Bunny look like it's got myxomatosis
On certain days he synchronises a single press-up with the
rising and falling of the sun

He jogs on the spot as I try my best to fall asleep
The sound of his exercise metronoming my dreams

Laughing to himself as he bench presses my gravestone

Every now and then Death falls silent
The bones of his feet stand lightly on the black
Something stops him on the spot
He stands confused with skeleton hands on skeleton hips
As appalled, as excited and as gobsmacked as I am
At what this world has to offer

Mobile Homes

Raindrops hang ready to drip from liquorice lines
When will they make the call to lay the word wires to rest?
Once strung up tunnels transporting busy trains of chatter from
house to house
I imagined words zooming through the lines like a news banner
If you cut them with secateurs
People's hearts would pour out of the end
Thin black hose pipes with words for water
Homes on the end of wires like static dogs made from brick
Telegraph poles for owners

Hay Wain

I settle on the leather sofa opposite
About five metres from the painting
If I had a stone
I wouldn't throw it
The oil paint has been drying since 1821
People stand in front and block my view
I marvel at the beauty of their rucksacks
The lines and fabrics of the zips and pockets come together to
signify a certain sense of security and a kind of modern take on
the intertwining NO!
Get out of the way before I smash your ears clean off with my
Van Gogh poster
The poster that I bought on the way in, just to make sure I had
something to look at
I wait until they move on
I am left with the painting
A lady places herself directly in front
Close up
So close she becomes part of the picture
Her head is now that of a sea serpent in the waters next to the
horse and cart
The workers are scared to life
They leap from the painting onto the wooden floor of the gallery
A coffin with pictures on the walls
They lie with their unpainted bones broken and twisted
The lady steps away from the picture
It returns to normal
Apart from the work element of the painting is no longer there
A supervisor arrives promptly and sweeps them up

Boombatch

There's this really famous photographer called Alfred Boombatch. You may not have heard of him because I just made him up. Boombatch takes extraordinary photographs of apples. They are not extra ordinary photographs of apples, they are extraordinary photographs of apples. What he does is he stands under apple trees at the time of year when all the apples are falling and takes thousands of photographs of the air under the apple trees, hoping that if he takes twenty thousand photographs in one day he will get at least one photograph with a falling apple captured in the frame.

An apple about to hit the earth of Earth.

Greeted with the kiss that leaves a bruise.

Alfred Boombatch has two photographs of apples.

Risks

I pickle risks and keep them in jam jars on my bookshelf
I look at the captured moment that I might have seized
Floating in the vinegar of my past
I think about unscrewing the lids and fishing them out
A risk I wasn't ready to take as a twenty year old
Seems manageable now
My jarred risks are skeletons of what was
Free from both danger and opportunity

Wedding Ringtone

A phone started ringing, but the ringtone was a recorded voice that repeated the sentence, My name is Stewart and I cheated on my wife. I looked around and could see a middle-aged man in a suit looking down at his phone. My name is Stewart and I cheated on my wife. My name is Stewart and I cheated on my wife. He let it ring and ring and then answered it.

Hi, yes I'm using the ringtone. No it wasn't on silent. Yes I'm on the bus, you knew I'd be on the bus at this time. Yes it's busy it's rush hour isn't it. What? Yes people heard it. What did they hear? You know what they heard. You want me to say it to you?

The top deck of the bus had fallen into silence. The man shut his eyes.

My name is Stewart and I cheated on my wife. Yep, OK, see you in about half an hour.

The man put his phone in his pocket, swallowed and looked out of the window.

Just as the conversations on the top deck of the 48 reignited Stewart's phone began to ring again.

Brain Freeze

My mind is at exactly the right temperature today
I can feel it
If I open my mouth for too long on a winter's day
My brain gets cold
I have to put layers on in my memories
I see myself as a six year old
Sitting on a beach in the almost blistering Portugal sunshine
Eating a Tom and Jerry ice lolly
Wearing a woolly jumper and bobble hat

Tattoo

When did you say you are getting your new tattoo finished?

I am going to get it finished before the winter for sure.

What is your new tattoo going to be of when it's finished?

I'm having a sheepskin coat done.

Whereabouts?

Where you would normally have a sheepskin coat.
I like to keep warm in winter.

But it would be a picture of a sheepskin coat wouldn't it?
Not an actual sheepskin coat.
Ink doesn't keep you warm.

Course it does, haven't you ever read a book?

Petrol Honey

In the supermarket that feeds the cars
The lady beeps my shopping closer to me
When my basket has returned to empty and my bags are full
The words move from her to me
Petrol honey?
Pardon?
Petrol honey?
Petrol honey?
Petrol honey
Petrol
Honey
Petrol honey IT SOUNDS LIKE WHAT IT IS
THAT IS WHAT IT IS
PETROL HONEY
YOU NEED THE PETROL TO MAKE THE HONEY
PETROL HONEY
YOU CAN'T MAKE THE HONEY WITHOUT THE PETROL
PETROL HONEY
THAT'S IT
Petrol honey
I start crying
There is a queue
Petrol honey
I pay
I leave

FORT FOR THE DAY

Steps

One morning I found a small piece of night sky that had fallen to Earth. At first I thought it was a curled up black cat or a dropped coat but it wasn't moving and it didn't have a tail. I lowered my hand to where I thought its mouth might be and to my surprise I could feel the cold breath of night on my palm. With nobody else around I went to stroke it and as I touched it I suddenly felt very tired as if it was the middle of the night. It isn't the dark that makes you feel tired is it? It's how long you have been awake for and what you've been doing. The instant tiredness was so real that I knew if I kept touching it I would fall asleep. So with nobody else around, I put my hands behind my back, knelt down and whispered, are you hungry? In a bold accent-free voice the night sky began to speak.

Err yes I am. I am very hungry. I am very, very hungry actually.

A darker area of black shape had appeared making a mouth with tiny stars for teeth. The fallen piece of sky began to talk to me like I was working for it. Ordering me about.

I am very hungry. Get me some food.

What do you eat? I asked.

What do you think I eat?

I don't know. I've never cooked for the sky before.

I eat the daytime don't I. Now go and buy me a nice juicy piece of daytime that I can eat will you.

What? How am I supposed to do that?

Don't you know? I eat day time like you eat chicken. If I want a snack I have quarter of an hour like quarter of a chicken. Half a chicken is half an hour and a full chicken is...

An hour? I interrupted.

Yes, well done you idiot. Now I want a full hour. An hour. What time is it now anyway?

WHAT? I shouted. I don't know what this is. What are you talking about eating daytime? Nighttime eating daytime. I don't get it. I don't understand. I was walking to the supermarket to get some milk and now this.

What's to understand? You seem to accept everything else in

this world easily enough without questioning it don't you? What do you mean? It's all I know. It's what I've been born into.

Yeah, but what about all that stuff that people tell you that you just take as gospel? Blue sky isn't blue sky it's just the science in your eyes telling you it's blue, red sky isn't red, jeans aren't jeans, they are just atoms that you wear on your legs. You've got all these people telling you what to do and what's real when they aren't even that sure themselves. You know in your heart that when you look up into the sky there is no lid. It just keeps going and going forever and ever and ever and it's infinite in each direction and that means that feeling in your chest, that is the centre of the universe. You are the centre of space that goes on FOREVER and you are letting all these people tell you what life is? Don't you think you should have a go at working it out for yourself? To live how you want to live?

What? NO SHUT UP I'VE GOT COUNCIL TAX BILLS. I went to kick the night sky as hard as I could but my foot went right through it and fell asleep. I collapsed onto the pavement and lay on my back looking up to the blue of the morning and I began to think about everything that the piece of sky had said to me, and in an attempt to get up into the sky and eventually reach the moon to get a better view of the Earth, I took every upward step I had ever made and stuck them together to create a staircase of my past climbs. So every time in my life that I had climbed up onto say, a kick stool, the height I climbed would be represented by that particular kick stool, one kick stool for every time I climbed up onto it. These were then stuck together with some sort of strong bracket resulting in a narrow set of stairs made entirely from kick stools. Having worked in an art supplies shop for three years I had stood up on the same red kick stool thousands and thousands of times. I watched as the red kick stool climbs were fixed together by a construction team of people that seemed to appear from nowhere, who all wanted to help me with my task of getting above the clouds and reaching the moon. Before I knew it there was this thin staircase of kick stools disappearing up into the sky with stanchions. I then began to think of all the ladders I had climbed over the course of my life and saw them appear instantly above me. Ladders from back home in York when Dad sent me up into the loft to get the Christmas decorations down. Wooden ladders and metal ladders of all sizes came together to give me another couple of kilometres of height.

Then came the stairs of my life. I began to think about every stair and staircase I had climbed since birth. Starting with the stairs that I tried to climb when I was a baby, the stairs I was too small to climb, the ones that my parents helped me up by holding my hand. Then the stairs to my upstairs flat in Walthamstow. Climbing them almost every day for the past three years, that has to be at least eight hundred stair climbs, and then the stairs to my university flat in Newcastle, the stairs to my halls of residence, the stairs to every upper deck of a bus I have ever travelled on, the three or so stairs to the National Express coaches, the purple wooden steps up to the waltzers at the village fair I used to save up for as a child, the odd spiral staircase, the stone steps of every major city I have ever visited. Seeing all the steps being stuck together from end to end to end to end to end I was surprised at just how high they went.

I looked up to see the structure now with clouds passing across it and began to think I may actually complete the 384,400 km journey to the moon.

Next came my escalator trips, London underground stations, the trips to Marks and Spencers with my Mum when I was little. Metal upon metal was fixed together as the world's media began to gather at the base of my upward climb.

Why are you doing this? they asked.
Why aren't you doing this? I replied.

Next a huge elevator shaft was built. The Empire State building gave generously. As months of construction passed they all added up and up and up and up and I began to realise just how unsteady the structure looked. Like an outdoor staircase built by Tim Burton with Edward Scissorhands as his head architect. Jagged and bad teeth like. Swaying in the wind.

I tried to tell myself that I have climbed all these before. I can do it again.

People started to really want to help me, they would all come with memories of stairs that we had climbed together, stairs from football grounds, theme parks, car parks.

When people stopped offering up information, I packed a bag, said my goodbyes, left my phone on the kitchen table and began to climb up the red kick stools of my past. Voices from the art shop filled my head as I quickly rose up into the morning sky. Pretty much every minute I spent in that shop, I thought I wanted to be somewhere else. Now I was somewhere else, and I still didn't know where I wanted to be. I had always been afraid of heights but this just seemed different in some way. Like I was climbing up a memory that was never going to let me fall. Or maybe I was climbing up my own life. That is what I've got to do I thought. Climb up my own life until I die. Different steps came with different memories. I knew I had climbed steps with my Grandpa but couldn't remember them.

After a couple of years of climbing I finally reached my destination. I had done that thing when you climb a hill and say, don't look round at the view until we reach the top. When I stepped foot on the moon my foot plummeted into its dust up to my knee. I felt a long way away from war and love and my friends and my family. I lifted my moondust coated foot and looked round at the ball where I live and could almost see the beautiful birds flying around it. I stood there for a minute in silence, took a deep breath, and began to make my way home on all the downward journeys I had ever made.

On my return I realised that all the magic has been done down here. The beautiful, horrific, bumbling, inspirational, unorganised chaos that is the human race on planet Earth. We only see the sun rise because the Earth gives it something to rise from. The birds only fly because they've got something to land on. What is the sky without someone to look at it, and someone to look at it with?

The sky is the topping but the earth is the cake.

Every time I go up in a plane I look forward to being above the clouds but I feel such a sense of relief when I get my feet on the ground.

I know I am back where I belong with the species I belong to. Where I can say the words, *the sky*, and people know what I mean.

If the world is a stage then the sky is the backdrop and I don't know what kind of a messed up comedy drama this life is but I do know that this is my home, this is where I need to be, and whenever life gets too much, I can look up and escape to where life isn't, to prepare myself for where life is. The sky is as blank as the future, the past is littered with what we've done but the future is clear, as clear as when you look up and you can't see where it stops. I guess that's where the phrase, *the sky's the limit*, comes from. There is nothing to stop you.

ARE YOU THE ORANGUTAN WHO SAYS "YES" ALL THE TIME?